Gil Walsh Interiors

Gil Walsh Interiors
A CASE FOR COLOR

GIL WALSH
with Margaret Reilly Muldoon

GIBBS SMITH
TO ENRICH AND INSPIRE HUMANKIND

For my mother, Mary Gill Moran

20 19 18 17 16   5 4 3 2 1

Text © 2016 Gil Walsh
Photograph credits on page 192

Published by
Gibbs Smith
P.O. Box 667
Layton, Utah 84041

1.800.835.4993 orders
www.gibbs-smith.com

Jacket designed by Debra McQuiston
Interiors designed by Renee Bond
Printed and bound in Hong Kong

Gibbs Smith books are printed on either recycled, 100% post-consumer waste, FSC-certified papers or on paper produced from sustainable PEFC-certified forest/ controlled wood source. Learn more at www.pefc.org.

Library of Congress Control Number: 2016933255
ISBN: 978-1-4236-4168-1

Contents

Foreword

by Steven Stolman

I am not now, nor have I ever been, an interior designer. But I have lived among and worked with many and like to think that I know a beautiful room when I see it.

Gil Walsh, the design firm, also knows a thing or two about beautiful rooms, because they create them. With painstaking attention to detail, unabashed use of color, and a deep knowledge of the history and traditions of interior decor, they have delivered extraordinary comfort and style to their clients. That is evident in the gorgeous photographs within this inspiring book.

Gil Walsh, the lady, conjures up a very different kind of beauty. When I first met her years ago in Palm Beach, and to this day, I have always been impressed by her ability to take the ordinary and make it extraordinary. Stuff like a shirt, a bracelet, a pair of spectacles—on everyone else, they remain just that: stuff. But on Gil, everything seems special.

Call it spirit, chic, joie de vivre, whatever, this is what Gil brings to the rooms lucky enough to receive her artistic touch. And that's a beautiful sight to behold.

Preface

by Margaret Reilly Muldoon

Sixteen years ago I had the pleasure and good fortune of being introduced to Gil Walsh by my sister. We met atop the D&D Building in Manhattan, where we were having lunch. The two of them were in town shopping for my sister's new apartment at the UN Plaza.

I was immediately taken with Gil's personal sense of style and how she saw color both in her wardrobe and the images from her work. At the time, Gil was heading the interior design department of a large Pittsburgh-based architectural/engineering firm. She recognized the potential of the Florida real estate market and convinced the firm to open a West Palm Beach office. It was an immediate success. Her Pittsburgh clients were making the move to Florida as seasonal residents, and a whole new group of homeowners began to see her work and commission her services.

Meanwhile, I moved to the Palm Beach area after more than twenty years heading my own communications firm in New York City. Gil introduced me to her firm and I was hired to handle the publicity and special events.

When Gil struck out on her own, I went with her, and the rest is history. It has been an amazing and exciting time watching the growth of Gil Walsh Interiors and the evolution of her style and work for clients up and down the East Coast, from Martha's Vineyard to the Keys.

When asked to write this book with Gil, I immediately agreed. I knew that her work merited a book and the time was right. *Gil Walsh Interiors: A Case For Color* is a selection of Gil's work over a twenty-year period. Each image brings to life her wonderful artistry and the inspiring and dramatic looks she has achieved for her clients. It has been an honor to help introduce her ideas to lovers of interior design and designer monographs everywhere.

Introduction

by Gil Walsh

My career in interior design began by way of my parents and grandparents, who taught me to love art, music, and design in a wonderful upper middle class background. We often visited nearby Pittsburgh, where my mother, Mary, took us to museums and the symphony.

Both my father, Thomas Wesley Moran Jr., and his father were physicians who practiced in Latrobe, Pennsylvania, a small mill town of 11,000 plus people. Grandfather Moran was a superb violinist and singer. He had a keen interest in beautiful furniture and furnishings, so I was surrounded by exquisite objects while growing up. We are all influenced in the direction our lives take when we are young, and I feel so blessed to have had a wonderful childhood with my large extended family—lots of cousins and doting parents and grandparents—and noisy family dinners. We were three children in my family, two girls and a boy.

As Dad practiced medicine, Mother studied art. Mother had a wonderful eye and great style. A painter, she was originally interested in realism but later changed her focus to contemporary art. She took art classes, driving forty miles to Pittsburgh with my sister and me in tow, enrolling us in small art programs at the museum. Our wonderful outings gave me an appreciation for art, culture, architecture, and design. My sister, Julie, has become a private fine art advisor in New York City.

Mother's father, James Gill, was a self-made man who ran a steel company. Latrobe was surrounded by steel mills, providing work for hundreds and the eventual fortunes of a select few, like the Carnegies. My name was derived from a combining of my mother's first name with her maiden name, Gill; she changed my spelling to Marigil, and I am called Gil, for short.

Back in the 1930s, Grandfather hired an interior designer from Pittsburgh, something unheard of in Latrobe. I inherited his love for jewelry, furniture, and lush flowering gardens, spurring my initial interest in botanicals. Gardens have always played a part in my overall concept of design. His garden was a beautiful haven for me as a child.

My father served in a MASH unit in the Army and the Naval Medical Corps during the Korean War. After his discharge, our family moved to Boston before our move back to Latrobe. My parents built a classic-style house of red and pink brick with black shutters next door to Winnie and Arnold Palmer, their lifelong friends. As the first-ever debutante from Latrobe, I received considerable press coverage at the 1969 Cinderella Ball, thanks to the presence of the Palmers.

In his day, Arnold Palmer was ranked top in the golf world. Arnie learned the game from his father, who eventually became the pro at the Latrobe Country Club.

Palmer was later a founder of Laurel Valley Golf Club in Ligonier, Pennsylvania, and represented the club on the PGA tour. Years later, Palmer commissioned me to do the interior design renovations on the guest bedrooms in the Palmer Pavilion at Laurel Valley.

As my parents' house was being built, my mother hired an interior design firm from Cleveland to decorate it in a traditional English style, with chintz upholstery. The beautiful wood furniture and colorful fabrics set my imagination to work. I began to take an interest in all things involving design, hoping to educate myself with magazines and books. My education, in fact, was very liberal. It was the 1970s, and the Vietnam War was on, but in the States life was fun, with few restrictions. You can only attend so many rock concerts before your parents question whether or not you have any thought to the future. After my freshman year at Latrobe High School, I went to Oldfields, the boarding school in Maryland that Wallis Simpson attended. Starting my formal education at a junior college in Millbrook, New York, I studied fashion design at Bennett College and finished my education at Chatham College then went on to the Art Institute of Pittsburgh for a Fine Arts degree. I wasn't ready to declare a major but loved drama classes. I designed all the sets and costumes for an avant-garde production of a play written by Pablo Picasso. I realized

that creating sets struck a passionate chord in me—a three dimensional world that my eye and brain understood. A budding interior designer was about to bloom.

Where to go and how to get started in this career? I scheduled an interview with Irvin & Company in Cleveland. They would come to play an important role in my life. To get to my interview, Winnie and Arnold Palmer offered me a ride on their private plane that was taking them to the Firestone Classic in Ohio. While looking for an apartment, I lived with Arnold Palmer's agent, Mark McCormack. Mark and his wife, Nancy, introduced to me realtors and people at country clubs, including the Marotta family (inventors of Mr. Coffee), along with Vincent Marotta and Art Modell, co-owners of the Cleveland Browns. Art's wife, Patricia, was an actress on *General Hospital.* They introduced me to their friends, and I was hired on my first big design project. In the midst of everything, I found the time to marry my college sweetheart, who was training in thorax surgery in Cleveland. I was thrilled by all my good fortune. I was on my way!

Hired as an assistant designer by Irvin & Company, the firm that had decorated my parents' house, I was now working at the largest interior design firm between Chicago and New York. They had their own workrooms, drapery, lamp shade and refinishing shops, along with electricians, warehousing, and delivery people. At Irvin & Company, weekly classes were taught about scale, upholstery, period furniture, lighting, and architecture. I also took night classes for two years in drafting while learning from the owner of the company about how to sell to clients.

There was not a design magazine I didn't buy. As I began to make more money, I purchased interior design books. My middle-class background also afforded me wonderful trips with my family to Europe and around the United States. We visited museums, looked at superb art and buildings in various architectural styles, some dating back centuries. I wanted to know as much as I could and wanted to soak up all the knowledge immediately.

But there are always steps, and I began to study individual elements such as fireplaces, staircases, entertainment centers, bookcases, skirted dressing tables, sofas and chairs, rugs, draperies, lamps, shades, folding screens, tile, wood, and hand-painted floors. I began to think conceptually about how to design a room that fits the lifestyle of its owners. How do you create a library or den? How do you design a room to be functional yet stylish? I felt drawn to interior design concepts for coastal homes, historical houses, and Florida-based condos and homes.

I read articles on how to repair wood and fabrics and created my own reference library over the years on these and other important topics. It has proven invaluable to my design team and me on so many occasions. Knowing how the inside works with the outside is the first step in a successful job.

While working in Cleveland, I was contacted by Cordelia Scaife of the Mellon family at the suggestion of my mother's great friend Brownie Saxman. Brownie was a smart businesswoman. Her friend Cordy, however, preferred to stay out of the limelight to such a degree that when she bought the Nemacolin Inn she preferred to work with a firm outside of Pittsburgh. An avid preservationist, Mrs. Scaife purchased this 2,000-acre resort in the Laurel Highlands and hired me to do the redesign. Today the resort has changed dramatically under new ownership.

Mason Walsh was a client who brought me to western Pennsylvania to decorate his home in Ligonier. As both our first marriages had ended, we began to date and married in 1982. That turned out to be the best job of my life!

FACING, LEFT TO RIGHT: Grandparents Moran's house. Grandparents Gill's house.

Mason introduced me to John Oliver, president of the Western Conservancy, who asked if I would be interested in working with Edgar Kaufmann Jr. on refurbishing the interiors of Fallingwater, Frank Lloyd Wright's masterpiece considered by many the greatest single family home designed in the twentieth century. I was initially hesitant to accept, since I didn't have an extensive knowledge of Wright's work. I had studied classical architecture but not organic, the school that Wright subscribed to. Mason suggested that I learn, and that's what I did. I met a man who had many of the original books written on Fallingwater and Frank Lloyd Wright. Through them I was able to begin to understand Wright's process and how he worked. (You will find more of this story starting on page 100).

When Mason retired as the personal attorney to the Mellon family, we bought a home in Jupiter, Florida. I commuted a great deal since I was heading the interior design department of a large Pittsburgh architectural/engineering firm. Mason traveled back and forth to our home in Ligonier, Pennsylvania, to take advantage of the bird-hunting season. We had three dogs—great hunters and the love of our lives outside of Mason's two marvelous children from his first marriage. Today I am the proud grandmother of five. Mason and I were spending so much time in Florida, though, that I suggested to the Pittsburgh firm that we open a Florida office for architecture and interior design.

After a period of time, I decided to strike out on my own and set up Gil Walsh Interiors (GWI) in Northwood, West Palm Beach, and I never looked back. It was a risky time to start a business in 2008, after the collapse of the stock market, but the success has been worth all the tears and fears. I sold my designer clothes and jewelry to help finance the company, literally giving the shirt off my back to start the business. The return has been overwhelmingly rewarding.

The office is a jewel. I love the clean lines of the polished chrome-and-glass desks and tables and the sparkling white walls and furniture. I have a great team of a dozen smart, ambitious talented full-time employees who are delighted to work with our clients (plus seven part timers for PR, social media, website design, marketing and accounting). We collaborate on all projects and together created our company motto: "Passionate visionaries collaborating with clients to make environments that evoke comfort, function and style."

If asked to define my design philosophy, I find it difficult to confine my answer to one style. I am classically trained, studied every period of furniture, every style of architecture, French, Italian and English. I have absorbed incredible works of art in my travels, gaining inspiration from the masters, the impressionists, the surrealists and the contemporary art world. I work in traditional, period, contemporary and modern interior design. I am the sum total of all of these disciplines. I believe in color—bright, vivid, brilliant, subtle, or demure color. I believe that color is the difference between bland, boring space and *a room*. One should never be overt, but one should never be timid. In a word, I am a colorist.

My ambition is to continue to learn and master my art, to bring vibrancy and a chic individuality to my world and yours.

TOP, LEFT TO RIGHT: My father, Thomas Moran, in his naval uniform during the Korean War. My husband Mason with Grandmother Julia Moran, my father's mother.

CENTER, LEFT TO RIGHT: The Walsh clan together in Martha's Vineyard with my mother, Mary Moran, on the left. Me at the Vineyard.

BOTTOM, LEFT TO RIGHT: Me with Holly, Max, and Spruce. Me with grandsons Duncan, Bayard, and Theo.

Top, LEFT TO RIGHT: Mary and Tom Moran with Kit and Arnold Palmer. Sister Julie and me on Easter Sunday. My parents, Mary and Tom Moran.

CENTER, LEFT TO RIGHT: Me and Mason. Sister, Julie Moran Graham, with her husband, Robin Graham; me with our dog Lily, and Mason. Me being presented at the Cinderella Ball in Pittsburgh.

BOTTOM, LEFT TO RIGHT: Mason with grandchildren Neva and Aksel. Me with boarding school classmates at Oldfields School.

TOP, LEFT TO RIGHT: Attending a White House luncheon with First Lady Nancy Reagan. Me seated, with (left to right) Aunt Lucille Gill, my mother, Mary, and Grandmother Gill.

CENTER, LEFT TO RIGHT: My younger days. Mary and

Tom Moran flanking Arnold Palmer. Julie and me with Grandfather Gill.

BOTTOM, LEFT TO RIGHT: Me and Mason on vacation, Me, Julie, and our brother, Tom. Dad and me on my wedding day.

Lush Layering

Layers give depth, and depth is the difference between a space with furniture and a finished room.

When you look at classical architecture, your eye is struck by the visual effect of the brickwork, the placement of cornices and plaster ornamentation, a wrought iron door, or a rococo balcony. These layers of brick and mortar identify the architectural style. The intricate motifs distinguish a classical building from a simple box building, although there is place in our appreciation for those as well. I love the fact that there is room for all styles of architecture—French, English, Italian, green and organic—as there is for personal preferences in décor—traditional, contemporary, Art Deco or modern. In every instance, layering makes a room distinctive, elegant, and welcoming.

Rooms come to life with color, contrast, and mixtures of period furniture and fabrics. One can make a simple sofa interesting by the addition of nailheads or a border of fringe. The mixing of styles and materials like antiques, Lucite, or lacquered furniture all become actors in this play we are producing, because we are setting the stage.

I work from the ground up or with art to start my color scheme. I might start with a Persian carpet, a woven silk rug from India, or a natural sisal rug. This is the foundation. A rug becomes the stage on which to build and centers your room to become the first scene of an award-winning production.

The entrance to my Jupiter home, accented by a trompe l'oeil, a painted chinoiserie chest, circa 1930s wrought iron chairs, all anchored by reclaimed wood columns and a carved wood chandelier.

A Palm Beach mansion is a mix of French, English, and Italian pieces. Custom-designed area rug by Gil Walsh Interiors. A hand-painted wood buffet chest anchored by two Louis XVI painted bergère chairs looks perfect against beige-and-white striated walls.

ABOVE: Overview of the Palm Beach living room with Italian glass-and-faux-marble bunching tables facing French gilt metal mid-century Maison Jansen glass coffee table. Two 18th-century wheel-back chairs are painted black and covered in blue-and-white fabric. The pair of custom sofas bordered in blue coordinates with the custom-made area rug.

Right: The scope of this Martha's Vineyard shingled house is a designer's dream. I worked in tandem with the architect during the building process to ensure the owner's art collection would be prominently displayed throughout the house. The arch beamed ceiling of the great room enhanced its scale and grandeur, affording multiple sitting areas in the same color scheme.

Below: A sitting area off the second-floor gallery provided a wonderful showcase for the owners' priceless Americana art collection. A two-tiered spool table was placed below a framed collection of antique flags.

Working from a modern interpretation of an antique hook rug. The colors of red, blue, and gold are taken from the painting hanging to the right. The fireplace was designed by a local Martha's Vineyard artisan.

Rooms in the Ligonier, Pennsylvania, townhouse that my husband and I recently completed (pages 26–30) best illustrate my concept of lush layering. I must confess that I am an inveterate collector of furniture, all periods and styles, and I have a passion for chairs. You will find chairs everywhere in my homes—little chairs, big chairs, corner chairs . . . chairs! My furniture collection includes all periods and styles, some handed down from family.

I like mixing styles and woods. These pieces seem to complement each other rather like a League of Nations from France, England, Sweden, Ireland, and Asia, all sitting in one room and getting along perfectly with each other. I am never afraid the woods will clash; somehow they work in concert with each other. My personal choice often leans to the traditional, yet I adore the clean white and chrome of modern or contemporary tables and chairs, as my design studio in West Palm Beach, Florida, shows. Clean white shelves house fabric swatches, with cubbyholes for sketches and floor plans. The clear glass surface never distracts from the colors and fabrics I pull together for a client.

A good example of layering is my eclectic dining room with a true international influence. The furniture comes from various countries and periods yet works together in harmony. I began from the ground up with a natural sisal rug centered to lift all the layers to high style. The centerpiece is an inlay English Sheraton dining table bordered by primitive Hepplewhite English chairs and a reproduction French settee covered in natural muslin, with a fur throw. The backdrop is a dramatic choice of deep aubergine for the walls. This color choice just seems to enhance the stunning mahogany American breakfront and split Asian wood carved screens I collected along the way.

I wanted the eye to be drawn to the windows draped in blue-and-white silk plaid, permitting the natural light to catch the high polished sheen of the furniture. A white coffered ceiling elevated the room even more, just the right architectural touch I needed to dramatize the Swedish crystal chandelier. Naturally, there is a mix of color everywhere—on seat cushions and throw pillows in an array of coral, red, green, deep pink, and blue. The added touches include French porcelain plates in the breakfront, a pair of Venetian Blackamoor statues in front of the windows, and an American folk art swan on an antique chest.

LEFT: A true example of lush layering can be found in my eclectic Ligonier dining room, a combination of styles and periods, including a reproduction French settee, English Sheraton dining table, and Hepplewhite English chairs. The Swedish chandelier is suspended from a coffered ceiling. Blue-and-white-plaid silk drapes work in tandem with the deep aubergine walls.

ABOVE: Just off the dining room is my home office, with a reproduction of a 1970s Kittinger George Washington desk just below a portrait of me with the dogs. The upholstered chair is covered in a Colefax & Fowler chintz fabric, and a zebra skin rug finishes the room.

ABOVE: Our guest bedroom in Ligonier has a soft rose trellis–patterned wallpaper. The bed is done in an old Brunschwig & Fils floral print for the headboard, bed skirt, and valance. To the right, a Baker stacked chest. All centered on a natural woven rose wool-and-cotton carpet.

FACING: The guest powder room walls are done in a Zoffany rose cabbage print. The walnut cabinet is topped in sculpted Carrara marble, with whimsical bird fixtures from P. E. Guerin. The chandelier was reclaimed from an old Broadway theater.

A perfect example of my passion for chairs. Large or small, I adore them all. Many have been passed down in my family for generations, so they are particularly special to me.

The sofa should take center stage. I begin to layer the sofa with decorative pillows or a soft cashmere throw. Layering continues as I decide what color to paint or paper the walls; either one or both can bring in additional artistry by creating a backdrop that emphasizes the placement of the furniture. End tables and lamps are yet more layering. And lighting is critical in establishing the mood.

I think of designing a room like baking a cake. One vanilla layer is just that; it might as well be a plain pound cake. But add a layer of chocolate filling and another layer of cake and you have the beginning of something delicious. So think of your living room as a cake. Begin to envision what color icing you want and how you plan to decorate it. Add the ruby red color of fruit or the leafy green of a flower, and think how you will handle the decorative border. Then light it up with candles. Now you have a presentation to be applauded!

This Florida den began with an Oushak Turkish rug as the base for the color scheme. The huge windows command extraordinary views of the gardens. The soft blue chair and ottomans with coral accents complete the look of the room. To the right, a coral-and-white-striped wallpaper for the hallway leading to bedrooms.

FACING, TOP LEFT: Country English Tudor in western Pennsylvania. The artistry and colors of the area rug set the tone for the entire room. Oversized sofas in a butter yellow play with the rich burgundies and grays used throughout. The scope of the room, with its immense fieldstone fireplace and beamed cathedral ceiling, further dramatizes the Tudor style.

FACING, TOP RIGHT: Lush layering continues from the bottom up—starting with this brilliant Portuguese needlepoint rug of rose, green, blue, and gold—introducing an array of fabrics and soft color choices in solids, stripes, and damask. The blue-and-white-plaid silk drapes continue the color theme and add to the layered effect in this western Pennsylvania farmhouse.

FACING, MIDDLE RIGHT: Layering can begin with art or the wall treatment. In this elegant drawing room, the rose/coral wallpaper sets the tone for the rest of the room, including the French Aubusson carpet of rose, yellow, and celadon.

FACING, BOTTOM LEFT: An English dry bar becomes more interesting when surrounded by an eclectic group of pieces such as the French drawings and a pre-Raphaelite screen on the walls coupled with an Italian chest and hand-painted chairs by the famous British artisan Graham Carr.

FACING, BOTTOM RIGHT: From floor to ceiling, this exquisite dining room begins with a precious oriental carpet centering the room for the Regency table and damask-covered chairs. The striped silk drapes draw the eye to the magnificent patterned parquet ceiling.

ABOVE: Pale coral, white, and blue patterned carpet is showcased with white sofas and chairs throughout the room, accented with blue-and-white throw pills and coral panels of color set into the walls.

LEFT: This magical Suzani carpet strikes a colorful note in this Jupiter, Florida, home. An eclectic collection of art, furniture, and furnishings represents two separate lives lived over many years and now united in one home with a new marriage.

ABOVE: This Florida living room takes its direction from the superb Asian paneled screen, bringing the oriental carpet together with a silk velvet sofa and painted wheel-back chairs.

ABOVE: The Classic rotunda foyer in this Pennsylvania mansion is sure to stop traffic, from the limestone-patterned floor to the painted Gothic quatrefoil center table. The alcoves house a pair of Graham Carr chairs.

FACING: Another dramatic entrance is this two-story foyer in a Palm Beach County home. Because the ceiling is so high, we used a trompe l'oeil with climbing monkeys to fill the space. More layering comes from the oriental rug, English chest, Irish mirror, and English ladder-back chairs.

Jewel Tones

Jewels have a vibrancy and brilliance with their luster that captures the imagination.

Grandfather Gill was an avid gardener and a collector of gemstones. As a young girl, I was fascinated by the beauty of these stones and how refracted light changed their colors. Physicists call it "dispersion" when a white light passes through a prism and separates into its component colors—red, orange, yellow, green, blue, and violet. This prism of color can be the foundation for an elegant and richly layered room, permitting artificial or daylight to affect the color of walls, fabrics, furniture, and art.

Just as a flawless diamond in the right setting can produce a breathtaking effect, the same holds true when the right jewel tones are used in the living room, dining room, bedroom, or den.

When considering precious and semiprecious stones, it is important to understand there is a limitless spectrum of colors available, from moonstone to pale sapphire, amethyst, tourmaline, topaz, and aquamarine to the deep richness of the ruby, garnet, emerald, or onyx. Choosing a favorite gemstone color will transform a room into an elegant jewel, both precious and desirable to the eye.

Creating colorful vignettes in your home, or showcasing art, antiques, or a particular piece of fine furniture, is an impactful way to decorate. Each vignette becomes part of the entire scheme when you use color in wall coverings, fabrics, furniture, and accents to pull the room together for the story you want to tell.

You can take inspiration from nature, but I love taking my color inspiration from jewel tones—the palest aquamarines to the richest sapphires. The marquise cut is the perfect pattern in this multicolored jewel-tone fabric of ruby, sapphire, and coral, which mirrors the colors of the abstract painting.

ABOVE: The crowning jewel—a delightful settee covered in a vibrant floral print of red, blue, and gold. The side chairs are done in solid ruby red and sapphire blue for a perfect sitting area on a blue-and-white patterned rug. The painting over the settee is in perfect harmony with the room.

FACING: Color is the key for every room in the home, whether subtle or bold. A colorful settee in the dining area works well with a color coordinated fabric for the side chair and solid moonstone-colored dining chairs. The sweeping sheer valance makes the perfect frame for the window to the gardens.

A modern condo with pearl white sofas and strong accents of amethyst is further enhanced with artwork using bold splashes of orange, green, and red.

FACING: The combination of a strong yellow and blue makes this Florida living room come to life. A pair of ebony chairs in a honeycomb pattern reflect the dramatic colors of the painting above the fireplace.

ABOVE: Teal-and-moonstone patterned chairs fit perfectly in this Palm Beach living room. The silk moiré–covered sofas are accented with colorful blue and red patterned pillows.

ABOVE: The foyer of this Palm Beach home is done in a pale coral that cues from the oriental rug.

RIGHT: A pale sapphire bedroom glistens with a white quartz four-poster with matching duvet and headboard, creating a serenely pleasant way of bringing in airiness and light.

ABOVE: What could be more inviting than this vibrant coral and white dining room set for an elegant dinner party? Different woods on the dining table and the buffet shine like rare jewels.

FACING: A delightful foyer in this Florida home has a touch of whimsy with the combination of colors and patterns. The blending of golden yellow walls, a coral ceiling, and crown molding creates an amusing vignette.

Panels of color such as coral emphasize the architectural columns and beamed ceiling in this Florida residence. The use of white muslin for chairs and sofas, accented with blue in the pillows, along with the patterned rug demonstrate how the natural light from French doors plays an important architectural role in the room's overall dramatic effect.

ABOVE AND FACING: The same home greets guests with a pearl-and-onyx-tiled floor extending to the emerald carpeted stairwell and landing featuring a round garnet-and-sapphire-striped settee. Atop is a hand-painted pale blue-and-gray chinoiserie scene, bringing the subtle colors of nature into this exquisite neoclassic Pittsburgh mansion.

Color is the key for every room in the home. It can be dusty and subtle or bold and vibrant. Since the choice is yours, what you will create is a jewel, a precious and lustrous place that is as brilliant as its owner; a perfect gem that continues to delight the eye for years to come.

For inspiration, look in your closet and see where your eye takes you. It might be a fabulous red dress or a turquoise silk blouse that receives compliments every time you wear it. Now take those colors beyond your closet and surround yourself in their brilliance to create a dramatic series of rooms. Bring color into your life and you will bring magic into your world.

FACING: Pale amethyst walls make this bedroom special and inviting. The patterned rug adds more color and charm. The crisp white linen on the bed becomes even more luxurious with a fur throw.

ABOVE: This jewel of a master bedroom gets its beauty from the various jewel tones, much like the Imperial eggs commissioned by the Czar from the Russian jeweler Peter Carl Fabergé.

ABOVE: The pooling silk drapes of celadon and rose enhance the extraordinary bank of windows in this Palm Beach home. The coffered ceilings are painted pale green and white.

FACING, TOP: Continuing the pale semiprecious tones of green and white in the loggia is accomplished with a woven sofa and chairs covered in solid celadon cushions.

FACING, BOTTOM: Just as a flawless diamond in the right setting can produce a breathtaking effect, the same holds true for this bedroom of ruby-and-white floral patterns on a backdrop of canary yellow walls. The Aubusson carpet is an ideal marriage of style and taste.

Country Chic

I love *country houses* built near lakes, rivers, oceans
or in the mountains. My first country house memory
is the one my grandfather built that provided me with
a place to explore and *run free* in the summers.

When asked to design a country house or guest cottage, my mind immediately goes to how my client wants to use the house. I smile thinking of all the activities just outside the door—swimming, canoeing, croquet, hiking, sunbathing, dining, or just curling up with a good book.

The size of the house and its surroundings determine what will go inside and outside. Maybe it is a cunning cottage that is small in size but big on relaxation, or a large plantation designed for quail hunting. The ocean-front beach house calls for another approach to interior design, with multiple bedrooms for a growing family and children running in and out all day long from the ocean or pool; and space for dinners shared with family and friends, or gatherings in a den decorated with treasured family heirlooms. A real country kitchen is a special design element, where you can almost smell the bacon sizzling in the pan and where a breakfront is filled with china passed down from generation to generation.

A handmade quilt that might accent a child's bed doubles as a cloth for the table.

An airy and bright solarium is bordered by a white brick wall and French doors. The black-and-white marble floor adds a dramatic touch, while white muslin chairs and a pale green settee make a congenial conversation area. Moss green upholstered chairs, a Grecian-bordered white ottoman, and a mirror accented with metal straps make a cozy nook.

ABOVE: A painted breakfront filled with pottery made by the owner is the perfect background for a seaside living room. Artisan-blown globes collected over the years are among the owner's treasures.

FACING: Country chic can come in many looks, such as this French country chic foyer in a south Florida home. The floral wallpaper plays beautifully with a country French chest and the bold leopard-print area rug.

The style of the house determines how I approach the interior. For an intimate two-story shingled guest cottage in Palm Beach, I worked with the owner's treasure trove of art and decorative pieces, using wicker furniture on the wraparound screened porch and also in the living room, covered in vintage fabrics. The bold splashes of color played handsomely with the Hunt Slonem painting of tropical birds prominently positioned over the fireplace. My intention was to maintain the integrity of the house while modernizing the cottage for the comfort of guests, including an intimate tropical back patio for sunning and outdoor dining.

A house can come with a history, or a new history can begin with a new generation of owners. Memories are made each year as the stories are retold to new generations that gather.

This 1910 shingled cottage in Palm Beach enjoyed a long history of owners, such as the editor-in-chief of *House & Garden* and *House Beautiful* and its new owner, who wanted an intimate place for family and friends to enjoy the beauty and culture of Palm Beach.

Working in tandem with your environment is good design. A tropical climate should highlight the lush palm trees and flowering orchids and plants. In the deep country, the surrounding woods can set the tone for the style of furniture, such as Adirondack chairs or birch wood furniture for a feeling of Americana.

FACING AND ABOVE: A brick path leads to this lovely two-story Palm Beach cottage designed for guests and their comfort. The screened porch is filled with comfortable wicker furniture collected over the years by its owner. One of the two bedrooms in the cottage has the bed positioned on a sisal rug. An antique Americana quilt, simple grasscloth-covered nightstands, and nautical prints finish the look of the room.

The dining room of the guesthouse is designed for intimate dinners. McGuire bamboo chairs with colorful pillows surround a simple round table. The windowsill and bookshelves are filled with family treasures, pictures, ceramics, and books.

ABOVE: The bed in the second bedroom of the guesthouse is covered in a pale blue coverlet with matching pillows and ribbed pillow shams. The Venetian mirror in the corner is positioned near a mirrored chest, and the wall is covered with botanical pineapple prints for a true country chic look.

OVERLEAF: The back garden of the Palm Beach guesthouse is lush and welcoming with its tropical plants and palm trees. The wrought iron chaises, table, and chairs are done in Pompeii green, with Sunbrella fabrics for cushions and pillows—making the ideal place for leisurely outdoor dining.

The deep navy blue wall is the perfect backdrop to highlight the matching white sofas, with equal care taken in the private bedroom and bath.

Let your surroundings set the tone for what you do. A sophisticated Palm Beach mansion built in 1984 was designed with a private guesthouse fronted by the pool and bricked terrace. Guests can have their privacy while enjoying the lush tropical gardens only feet away, while the modern conveniences of TV and Wi-Fi are built in for maximum ease and comfort.

ABOVE: Guest bedroom with bamboo Palu four-poster spool bed covered in a Clarence House print for the duvet and shams. Wall-to-wall carpet, a three-drawer country chest, and a John Rosselli chair covered in a Pierre Frey fabric fill out the room.

OVERLEAF, LEFT: The dining room of Pineland Plantation with painted pecky cypress walls counter what is otherwise a formal dining room.

OVERLEAF, RIGHT: View of the 14-room two-story Georgian-style main house of Pineland Plantation. The grounds take up thousands of acres of land for quail and grouse shooting in Albany, Georgia.

The colors of nature can also set the theme for the colors used in your interiors, as in this Albany, Georgia, plantation set on thousands of acres of land. The two-story white Georgian-style main house dates back to the early twentieth century. It was originally designed to offer guests grouse and quail shooting during the season. The grounds are exquisite with stables, barns, and kennels situated throughout the property, which is expertly maintained following the centuries-old tradition of wagon and horses only, no cars.

The colors in the landscape helped determine the interior of this fourteen-room house: various shades of green with bold accents of red, blue, and gold in chintz fabrics for the living room and den. The master suite was done in a red/cream/blue floral chintz reminiscent of Marie Antoinette's boudoir in Versailles—without the ribbons.

The Pineland Plantation in Georgia has had only three owners since it was built around the 1930s. Its second owner, Lambert D. Johnson, expanded the property when he bought the estate next door from amateur golfer Bobby Jones, adding to the cachet and size of the estate.

The history of a house can also be provocative, as in the scandalous rumors surrounding Pineland's first owner, Judge Robert Worth Bingham. Following the sudden death of his second wife, Mary Lily Flagler—widow of Henry Morrison Flagler of Palm Beach and one of the wealthiest women in America—after only one year of marriage brought rumors of foul play by overdose or medical neglect. Although Mary Lily had changed her will, Bingham inherited a considerable fortune that enabled him to purchase the *Louisville Courier-Journal* and *Times*. With this influence and the wealth of his third wife, Bingham gained enough political clout to be awarded by FDR the ambassadorship to Great Britain in 1933. Oddly he was succeeded by seasonal Palm Beacher Joseph P. Kennedy, whose home was later known as the Palm Beach White House.

Regardless of where your home is located, with the right colors, fabrics, art, and heirlooms, you are bound to be country chic.

The ultimate in country chic is this extraordinary two-story white Georgian-style house dating to the early 20th century. Pineland Plantation was designed for grouse and quail hunting. Painted pecky cypress walls add a rustic charm to this foyer.

ABOVE: Overstuffed chairs in a chintz fabric take their color cue from the great outdoors on this Georgian plantation spread over thousands of acres of pristine land.

RIGHT: A feminine floral pattern was used for the matching headboard and bed skirt in the twin guest room. Striped wallpaper adds another layer and dimension to the room.

By the Sea

Seaside houses offer a *wide range* of possibilities and allow the use of bright, vivid colors to contrast brilliantly with a *clear sky*.

Because I was born in a mill town in Pennsylvania, a trip to the sea was always a treat. My husband and I began vacationing in Martha's Vineyard in 1985, acquiring an old hunting cottage four years later on a bluff overlooking Chilmark Pond. It was a wonderful refuge. As time went on and the family grew, in 2006 we realized our dream of building a larger house. We kept the original house for the children.

Designing the new house from the ground up was a great experience and thrilled my architectural heart. It allowed me to be a participant in every facet of the planning. An important role in my job as an interior designer is learning from clients how they want to live in and use their homes. I knew exactly what our family wanted and all of our individual preferences.

Kitchens are the place where family seems to gravitate, and that was to become an important room for us. We adore clean white cabinets and prefer white countertops for informal snacking or cocktails. When the kitchen is designed to extend out to an informal room for family and friends, the cook is never left out of the conversation.

Taking a cue from the blue of the sky and the white sandy beach, I decorated the living room in blue and white, with bright accents of red and yellow. A blue-and-white carpet became the first of many layers. As sofas, chairs, and tables were selected, their clean lines transformed the room into a seemingly effortless look of casual seaside chic.

A bobbin chair covered in a white cotton fabric and the drop leaf table are in the corner of my Martha's Vineyard living room. Accents like a blue and white bird-print pillow add cheer to the room. Homes by the sea can range from casual to opulent.

FACING: I adore my all-white kitchen. It's a place where the family likes to gather for snacks and cocktails or casual meals.

ABOVE: I took a casual approach for our Martha's Vineyard sitting room, working with cerused oak sofas and chairs. A Tibetan painted chest doubles as a coffee table. On the wall I hung ceramic animal figures and added an Amish barn star.

Seaside houses and condos offer a wide range of interior design possibilities and allow the use of bright, vivid colors to contrast brilliantly with a clear sky. Though the architecture is different from house to house, the options for an interior designer are endless. I love a cedar-shingled bungalow filled with family treasures as well as a multilevel stone house to showcase a priceless collection of Americana.

An oceanfront duplex in Boca Raton provided a unique opportunity to depart from the traditional look of the downstairs and design a riotous explosion of color in the Moroccan-inspired guest quarters in reds and purples bringing to mind the excitement of a North African bazaar. Three daybeds covered in hand-dyed fabrics with accent pillows are a thrilling departure and a fun place for all to lounge, since it led out to the roof-top terrace and built-in barbecue.

FACING: Another casual approach is the screened porch on this Palm Beach cottage. The wicker furniture covered with light, sunny fabrics adds a country feel. The wrought iron tables and chairs are both decorative and practical for indoor/outdoor living. Lattice obelisks bring height and interest to the setting.

ABOVE: The second floor of this Boca Raton oceanfront condo was converted into a guest suite. The daybeds covered in rich printed silks of vibrant gold, reds, and purples might be found in Morocco. It sleeps three.

FACING: The roof terrace of the duplex doubles as a private sun deck and outdoor dining area.

ABOVE: A large oval sun chair with bright orange-and-gold throw pillows adds sophistication to the terrace.

One of the headiest experiences I have had was helping a new owner to bring a neoclassic three-story Regency-style mansion in the estate section of Palm Beach back to its original beauty. Having been built in 1940 by Clarence Mack, its royal lineage began in 1952. Though it was on the verge of near collapse when the new owner purchased it, the house had much to distinguish it, including its historical designation. As with other houses in Palm Beach, the who's who list of former owners ran the gamut from dame to duchess to princess. Fortunately, the new owner had lived abroad for a number of years and had acquired some stunning period art and furniture that was perfect for a historical masterpiece.

A formal reception hall hand-painted in an old English maritime scene greets guests before they enter the French-inspired grand salon of pale green silk sofas, chairs, and drapes, making this one of the most elegant drawing rooms in town.

The dining room is very English, with a Regency-style table and chairs. The artwork included period portraits the owner had found in England, tying the theme together for an enchanting sense of sophistication.

LEFT: The cabana of this 1940s Palm Beach home provides a covered dining area for cocktails and casual meals. The gracious staircase leads to the loggia of this neoclassic Regency-style historic treasure.

OVERLEAF: The opulence of a Savonnerie carpet of pale celadon, rose, and gold becomes the centerpiece for this extraordinary French-inspired salon. Elegant fringe-bordered sofas and pale rose-and-green damask on the ottoman play beautifully with wheel-back chairs covered in a golden silk, resulting in one of the most charming drawing rooms in the estate section of Palm Beach.

FACING: A stunning English-style dining room boasts a Regency table surrounded by wheel-back chairs. Celadon silk drapes serve as a handsome backdrop for formal dinners. The portrait of a child hung above the buffet is a lovely addition to the room.

ABOVE: The interior of the cabana, with wrought iron chairs and white cushions, is the perfect location for relaxing with friends by the fireplace. The arched doorways add an important architectural element.

After such a heady project on an historical residence in Palm Beach, I wondered if I would ever be able to top that experience. The answer came by way of *Redemption*. Inspiration comes to me from art and nature and particularly from the sky and sea. What better way to fulfill a dream than to be commissioned to redecorate a yacht?

Built in 2004, *Redemption* is a spectacular 130-foot yacht capable of doing 21 knots. She has five en suite staterooms. Our firm was called in when she was refitted in 2015 at a shipyard located in West Palm Beach. As with so many yachts, the interior furnishings were all neutral tones, with beige carpeting throughout. Apart from the polished teak, nothing said "wow!" We added the wow factor with bright orange-and-white-striped ottomans, blue-and-white-striped bolsters on the upper deck, and colorful linens and bed covers in all the staterooms. We transformed the salon using colorful throws and accent pillows, putting a shine on this magnificent boat. The addition of bright orange throws transformed a lounge chair into a sunny place to be.

It reinforces my philosophy that color, either subtle or bright, can transform a room, a house, or a yacht into something wonderful to behold.

FACING: The opportunity to redecorate a 130-foot yacht, *Redemption*, brought two of my passions together: design and the sea. With five en suite staterooms and lots of outdoor decks, there was an abundance of places to add color and fashion touches to update this luxury ship.

ABOVE: Nautical navy blue and white stripes and solids get a splash of color with red/orange throws.

RIGHT: A twin guest bedroom is livened up with printed cotton and Hermes-like silk pillows on crisp white sheets.

BELOW: Who wouldn't want to sail the seven seas on this exquisite yacht? The master stateroom of high-polished teak is transformed into a luxurious bedroom with the addition of bright blue, gold, and red accessories and a throw.

FACING: The built-ins of polished teak seem more interesting with a Hermes throw and a toss pillow.

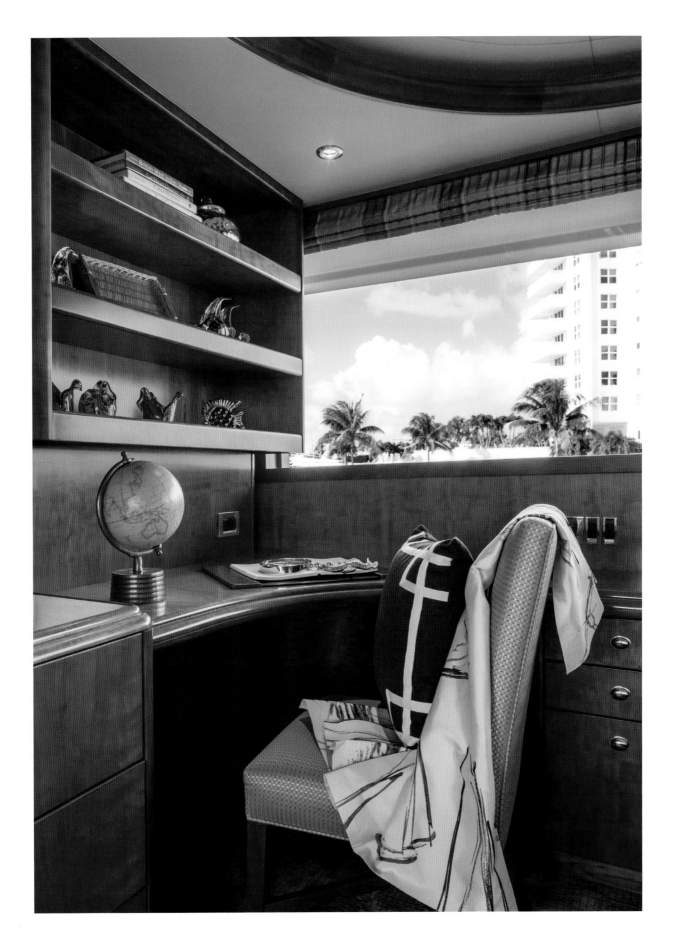

ABOVE: A Vero Beach patio becomes a second living room, with wicker furniture and striped cushions surrounding a mosaic tile coffee table.

FACING: A yellow clapper home in the Key West style on the west coast of Florida.

A seaside condo in South Florida has an elegance that starts with the terra-cotta floors and patterned rug. The sheen of the upholstered sofa contrasts beautifully with an animal-skin side chair. The dining chairs are covered in a burnt sienna silk stripe.

I created a side patio at my Florida home by laying Chicago brick. Distressed teak chairs covered in
a black-and-white stripe make for an enchanted sitting area, with lanterns hung or placed among the
potted plants and palm trees.

In the Clouds

As much as I *love* decorating houses, there is
something especially wonderful about a view of a
city or ocean from high *atop a high-rise*.

A duplex in Manhattan overlooking the East River and a condo on the Gulf in
Naples both offer unique vistas and ways of approaching interior design. Though I
love the serenity of a garden, there is something awe-inspiring about nature's influence on our views of everything—like looking out on the sea, how the color changes
with the tides, or how the setting sun transforms the interior of a room.

I feel so fortunate to have clients on both coasts and beyond. What comes to
mind is how spaces can be so different in décor. That is the wonder and excitement
of interior design, the opportunity to work in different mediums and architectural
styles. I cannot say I prefer one over the other, since each was special to me and
speaks to the individuality of its owner—always the ultimate goal. You will find two
distinct styles, representing French Moderne and eco-friendly, in these apartments
in the sky.

FACING: High up, overlooking the Atlantic Ocean, a living room of subtle blues and
whites matches the day sky. The room seems to float on a cloud, with handsomely tailored
sofa and accents pillows. The soft white walls and drapes continue the illusion.

ABOVE: The intricate design of this spiral staircase leading up to the guest quarters and roof terrace of a Boca Raton duplex is both practical and decorative.

FACING: The color scheme of rose and cream is used in both the living room and master bedroom. The handsome tufted settee is done in a linen floral toile. The high, coffered ceilings, crown molding, and pillars separate the living room from the dining area. A British colonial coffee table works well with the end tables, an antique chest, and stacked leather boxes.

In this master bedroom, the subtle pale rose and cream colors work beautifully in a floral print duvet with matching chair and ottoman. A white storage bench matches the covered headboard and frame, while white drapes frame a magnificent view of the Atlantic Ocean.

" . . . It was the nearest thing to heaven!" said Terry McKay in *An Affair to Remember,* starring Deborah Kerr and Cary Grant. You may recall that the scene had her looking up at the Empire State Building in New York City, about to meet and marry the man of her dreams. The immense pleasure seeing the Empire State Building and the abundance of architectural wonders in a city as varied as New York is indeed like a dream.

The UN Plaza encompasses two buildings, each a 38-story residential high-rise and running from the East River to First Avenue in Manhattan. Looking south, one is afforded a view of the United Nations and its gardens. On a clear day, one can see the New York Harbor and the Statue of Liberty. Originally built by Alcoa in the late 1960s, the UN Plaza has been home to the rich and famous—Truman Capote, Walter Cronkite, and Johnny Carson, just a few of the famous people who lived at the UN Plaza. The 3,300-square-foot duplex I was commissioned to decorate had been recently purchased by a now-retired CEO and Chairman of Mellon Financial Services.

Situated on the 35th and 36th floors, the space was almost entirely gutted, allowing the reconfiguring of certain rooms. We sealed off the back servants' staircase from the kitchen to create a separate fourth guest bedroom on the second level. The sweeping staircase from the front entrance was more than sufficient since the duplex included an elevator. The clients chose to decorate in the French Moderne style; not to be confused with Art Deco, French Moderne was France's term for modern furniture. This furniture was primarily custom made and shown in shops and galleries in Paris and Toulouse by makers and designers. What distinguishes this period are the beautiful and rare woods that were used in the furniture: tropical rosewood and ebony, along with sycamore and exquisite mahogany. American black walnut was also used. Furniture was often inlaid with mother-of-pearl or ivory, creating distinctive patterns. Although the Modern movement had been thriving throughout Europe since the early 1900s, its impact was delayed when the Paris exhibit was postponed due to World War I. Simultaneously, other influences came into being, such as the Egyptian revival, coinciding with the discovery of the tomb of King Tut in 1922, as well as Mayan and African influences, which played a part in the look and design of the period.

The colors chosen for the main salon, dining room, master suite and sitting room in this New York high-rise were various shades of beige for the sofas and chairs, accent pillows, and carpeting. The fabrics were silk moirés, jacquards, and beige-on-beige stripes playing to the wood grains of antique desks, tables, and bureaus purchased from dealers on the East Coast.

The sleek design of the sofas and chairs are in keeping with the whole Modern furniture movement. For counterbalance, I used simple wooden cocktail tables and a brass-and-glass console behind the sofa. I had a special screen made for the fireplace in brass in a deco motif. Each room had one authentic piece of antique French furniture, while good reproductions completed the end tables and furnishings for the dining room. A mix of materials included wrought iron and glass and dining chairs with an ebony finish.

We installed wall-to-wall carpeting throughout the main floor, and the upstairs corridor in a soft cream with a black border to dramatize the center hall staircase.

Since the clients were major art collectors and board members of several museums, including spearheading

The sweeping staircase in the foyer of this UN Plaza duplex is carpeted in beige wool, with a black border adding a more sophisticated look. The walls are treated to resemble marble. The desk is authentic French Moderne.

the fundraising, building and opening of the Warhol Museum in Pittsburgh, several Warhol pieces were selected for the home. In the living room, a portrait of Greta Garbo as Mata Hari from Andy Warhol's *The Stars from the Myths* series, acrylic and silkscreen ink on canvas, became the focal point and fit into the period furnishings. As a gesture to Mellon bank, the dining room has a deliciously colorful Andy Warhol piece entitled *Melons*.

The three guest rooms were done in black and white, using Donna Karan bed linens. The master bedroom had a custom-made bed and headboard and a quilted silk coverlet. The lighting showcased a superb men's bureau; the bed was anchored by a pair of period nightstands.

Even with three guest rooms, the sitting room of the master bedroom had pocket doors to afford privacy and additional sleeping quarters if necessary.

FACING: The stained white oak bar with a black granite top matches the storage cabinets for glasses and liquor in this French Modern-style high-rise apartment in Manhattan.

ABOVE: The table is set for a formal dinner. The dining room has two square tables to accommodate large and small dinner parties. Above the buffet table with a period coffee service is a painting by Hans Hofmann. Tortoiseshell boxes double as vases.

The night skyline of Manhattan can be seen from the formal dining room of this UN Plaza duplex apartment. The pedestal dining tables are replicas in the French Moderne style. The Andy Warhol painting, entitled *Melons,* is a tribute to its owner, the former CEO and Chairman of Mellon Financial Services.

The sitting room of the master suite is done in various shades of beige and taupe. The sitting room is separated from the bedroom by pocket doors, for privacy and also additional guest quarters. Painting by Kindred McLeary.

The living room is done entirely in the French Moderne style, with sleek lines on the sofas and chairs. The side chairs are walnut covered in a silk moiré. The fireplace screen was designed in brass and metal in a deco motif. The painting is of Greta Garbo as Mata Hari from Andy Warhol's *The Stars from the Myths Series,* acrylic and silkscreen ink on canvas.

The master bedroom has a custom-made bed with tufted headboard and platform. The bed is wrapped in a quilted silk coverlet. The gentleman's bureau is a superb original piece, and matching nightstands flank the bed.

The colors chosen for the main salon, dining room, master, and sitting room are various shades of beige. These two armchairs and the ottoman are covered in a beige jacquard fabric. The windowsills double as reading tables.

Sustainable design is more than a trend, rather a movement taken hold since the late twentieth century, in a manner an extension of the organic architecture of Frank Lloyd Wright. —Gil Walsh

TOP: The living room sofa and chairs are in soft butter leather in this SoHo-inspired loft in Naples, Florida. The owners had an eclectic art collection. The open floor scheme ensures space for the art both on walls and throughout. We employed a number of sustainable elements, such as bamboo flooring, a highly renewable resource.

CENTER, LEFT: A view into the dining area (left) and the living room (right) in this unique condo reveals that screens and curved walls serve to define various living areas. The dining room table, which is goatskin, is backed against a built-in banquette, with a painting by Jean Miró above. Toward the center is an interesting statue from the homeowners' collection.

CENTER, RIGHT: A metal screen becomes a room divider and provides the perfect location for this supine female sculpture. Pocket doors are used throughout the condo.

Although it was not possible to do an entirely sustainable condo in an existing high-rise in Naples, Florida, I was able to incorporate many of the ideas and practices that were both handsome in appearance and practical to the scheme of the project. I love organic and eco-friendly architecture, but it is rare to get the chance to use my training and certification in green design for interiors.

At purchase, this 4,800-square-foot condo was given over to the owners in what is termed "designer ready" (raw open space with only a finished kitchen and baths.) The entire condo had to be built-out and up. The open floor plan allowed the opportunity for me to devise curved walls and divide the living space with open grillwork and the placement of furniture to define areas for reading, watching TV, and dining. The beauty of this project was that the owners had a wonderful modern and eclectic art collection that needed a place to shine. Now retired, they wanted something minimalist, requiring little care and a total departure from the French country home they owned in Minnesota.

That simpler life began as I worked with a Florida west coast architectural firm to pull out all the cabinets in the kitchen and bathroom and redesign both areas with curved lava rock counters and the latest in low-energy appliances. Hiding the HVAC was an issue I had to solve, but the lighting system was a real challenge. Rather than lower the ceiling height, I devised a lighting system to look like a sculpture. Wanting to incorporate as many green elements as possible, I chose bamboo for the floors throughout the condo, a highly renewable natural resource. The large-plank flooring took on a life of its own, creating a natural pattern as an art gallery might employ.

The placement of the furniture defined the different living areas. I found a goat-skin dining table to complement the sleek minimalist look. By building a banquette, I was able to use the space more efficiently and open up an area on the back wall to show off a work by Joan Miró.

The owners had a massive Thai deity they always envisioned being by an outdoor pool. For their new home up in the clouds, I designed a fountain to serve as the statue's pedestal, making it intrinsically a focal point; water lilies complete the effect. Pocket doors were employed throughout to maintain the open space plan. Painting the foyer a deep red served as the entrance to a gallery for showcasing their art. The long hallway into the condo provided yet more space for art on cream-colored walls. Platforms were built for additional seating areas and served to elevate large sculptures.

The minimalist master bedroom was done in chocolate brown, accented by contemporary ebony cabinets and tables. The bedroom provided the setting for a painting by Eric Anfinson, a Minnesota fine artist whose work was part of the collection. The master bath has two paintings by Jamali, the originator of mystical expressionism. The art dictated the colors I used on walls as well as influenced the surfaces and design elements, which were selected with the goal of keeping the art as the primary focus.

It would be hard to determine just where this apartment is located if you didn't look outside and see the blue of the Gulf and the sway of palm trees. Florida condos are not usually known for this style of design. The idea of creating the look of a downtown SoHo loft was a wonderful tribute to clients with a bold sense of style and the willingness to depart from the norm.

BOTTOM, LEFT: The Thai deity was originally considered for placement by an outdoor pool. Since the apartment is in the clouds, we designed a fountain complete with water lilies to serve as a pedestal.

BOTTOM, RIGHT: The condo was delivered "designer ready," meaning only the kitchen and baths were finished. We ripped these out and redesigned them with curved lava rock counters. The master bath has two Jamali paintings.

Historical Treasures

As people enter, they are immediately transported back to a time in *history* when a single family could own such a *remarkable* place.

Having been raised in the Pittsburgh area, I saw fine examples of architectural styles—Italianate, Georgian, Tudor, Federal, Romanesque Revival, Jacobean, and Colonial Revival—built with the immense fortunes made from coal and steel, along with financial empires built by the Mellons and Carnegies. I educated myself in all these styles and disciplines along with the appropriate period furniture, creating a vast library that held me in good stead when I was commissioned to oversee the redesign and refurbishing of three historical properties in Pennsylvania.

A winter view of Frank Lloyd Wright's masterpiece, Fallingwater, built on 1,600 preserved acres in western Pennsylvania.

Fallingwater

Edgar Kaufmann Jr. insisted there be no velvet stanchions to prohibit visitors from the true experience of what it was like to play, read, and relax in this extraordinary weekend retreat. As a member of its advisory board, the thrill of walking through Fallingwater never fails to excite. I have an eternal appreciation to have

been chosen to play a role in this wondrous project. If you have never seen Fallingwater outside of photographs, I encourage making the trip; it's sure to be one of your most cherished memories.

My first commission in the early 1980s came from Fallingwater's former owner, but now steward, Edgar

ABOVE: A view toward the dining area shows the rough-hewn sandstone walls and floor of polished stones quarried from the property. Treasures collected by the Kaufmanns from around the world are used throughout the house.

LEFT: The office with its built-in desk and bookshelves. Wright designed over 160 freestanding and built-in pieces of furniture for the main house and guest quarters.

The living room at Fallingwater had built-in sofas and chairs covered in a natural 100 percent woven monk's cloth, many dyed to a brilliant red and yellow for use on hassocks and zabutons to soften the contrast with the sandstone walls. Wright designed and conceived the placement of each piece of furniture.

Kaufmann Jr., to replicate the fabrics of the architectural masterpiece, Fallingwater designed by Frank Lloyd Wright.

The Kaufmanns had been owners of the successful department store business. In 1935 they engaged Frank Lloyd Wright to design their weekend house known as Fallingwater. Set on a 1,600-acre tract of land in western Pennsylvania, Fallingwater is considered by some as the greatest single family home ever built in the twentieth century.

Rather than design a house that looked out on the waterfall known as Bear Run, Wright conceived of erecting the house above Bear Run, letting the river literally run under the structure. He designed a retractable hatch to enable the rushing water to serve as a cooling system for the house; the Kaufmanns could also descend into the natural pool by this opening.

The Kaufmanns took possession of the house in 1937. In 1939 the guest and servants quarters were completed.

Fallingwater opened to the public after Edgar Kaufmann Jr. donated the house and land to the Western Pennsylvania Conservancy in 1963. Each year, 150,000 people visit this living museum. Edgar Jr. remained its steward to ensure the aesthetic integrity that Wright conceived in his original design, including the maintenance of 160 pieces of built-in and freestanding furniture that Wright designed.

John Oliver, president of the Western Pennsylvania Conservancy, approached my husband, Mason, who served on its board, and asked if I would be interested in refurnishing Fallingwater. I met with Edgar Jr., who took me on a walking tour of the house. It was raining and water was leaking through the roof. I told him the house would have to be fixed before my work could begin and suggested that he hire a curator. We had a subsequent meeting in his New York City apartment. There I was hired to refurbish the fabrics in the Fallingwater living and sleeping quarters. Edgar Jr. was very articulate and smart, with enormous good taste.

My assignment was to replicate, in as authentic a manner as possible, the upholstery and other fabrics that had suffered from rain and exposure to the elements. Much of the original seat and back cushions were done in monks cloth, a natural beige 100% woven cotton fabric used extensively on sofas, chairs, hassocks, and zabutons. For many of the pieces, the fabric had been dyed to a brilliant red and yellow to soften and contrast to the rough-hewn interior sandstone walls and polished stone floors quarried from the property.

The Kaufmanns used their wide collection of objets d'art—bowls, vases, tribal Moroccan rugs, fur throws, and other treasures amassed on their world travels—to decorate tables, book shelves, cabinets, and display cases throughout the main house and guest quarters.

For replicating some of these textiles, I was fortunate to find samples of the actual fabrics or commissioned replicas from weavers. I met with some of the classic fabric houses—Boris Kroll, Isabel Scott, and the textile artisan Jack Lenor Larsen—whose collections of fabrics represented the artistry of many countries and cultures. The use of 100% natural fabrics was in keeping with the organic and sustainable scheme of the entire project and critical for me in maintaining the original look of Wright's interior design scheme while refreshing the room interiors and making them more interesting to the eye.

Rather than designing the house to look out on the waterfall known as Bear Run, Wright conceived of erecting the house above Bear Run, letting the river literally run under the structure.

Glendorn

An extraordinary sense of peace and tranquility comes over you as you pass through the wrought iron gates of the Lodge at Glendorn. Once the private retreat of a wealthy oil magnate and his family, Glendorn, a 1,200-plus-acre retreat in Bradford, Pennsylvania, was built in the late 1920s and early 1930s by Clayton Dorn for his growing family. The Lodge at Glendorn is nestled on two sides by the Allegheny National Forest. It was opened to the public in 1995 by the Dorn descendants. In the late '90s Cliff Forrest purchased the property with plans to preserve the natural surroundings and update the original buildings, which had been lovingly designed and expanded over the years.

Guests quickly experience the aura of this bucolic paradise as they pass a flock of sheep before reaching the main gate. The mile-plus drive to the main Lodge crosses rivers and well-stocked trout streams. As people enter the all-redwood Big House with a cathedral ceilinged great hall—which was the scene of private concerts for the family and friends by such jazz greats as Louis Armstrong and Ella Fitzgerald—they are immediately transported back to a time in history when a single family could own such a remarkable place for the year-round outdoor activities of hiking, fly-fishing, skeet and trap shooting, horseback riding, cross-country skiing, and cozy family dinners. There is also a mosaic-tiled, 60-foot, spring-fed heated pool for guests to enjoy. Today, between 3,500 and 4,000 guests annually come to this once private estate.

An ongoing project, I began my work of refurbishing the Lodge and the outer buildings in 2013. Since no resort today can be without a spa, I set about utilizing one of the buildings to create a place of tranquility, using faux barn siding for the interior walls. Guests are pampered with a mani/pedi, facial, and massage. The baths have slate tiles and counters, continuing the rustic theme. Seating throughout is Adirondack style, made of bendable willow in soft hues of yellow and green.

I next tackled the bar and dining rooms, adding new carpets and wall and window treatments, and reupholstering the existing furniture and antiques. I wanted to keep the individual theme of each of the cottages, done in a way that harks back to its original theme while offering every comfort and amenity. The decor ranges from Early American to Palm Desert circa 1970, so there are an abundance of styles and periods to explore.

There are a total of twelve log and stone structures made up of cabins and guesthouses and over forty stone fireplaces throughout the buildings, including the two-story sandstone fireplace in the Big House.

Each guest cabin reflects the style and personality originally designed and decorated by a member of the family. The most famous, and first to have been built is The Roost, a three-bedroom guesthouse with his and her baths. The Lodge is filled with treasures collected over the years and prominently displayed throughout. A grand stairway leads to the balcony and four guest suites. What could be more satisfying to an interior designer's heart than a quintessential compound of log cabins in the woods?

The picturesque landscape of Glendorn with its well-stocked trout stream was once the private 1,200-plus-acre estate of the Dorn family in Bradford, Pennsylvania, nestled on two sides in the mountains of the Allegheny National Forest.

LEFT: The relaxation room at the spa at Glendorn with bendable willow furniture in the Adirondack style. The fireplace and mantel was redesigned by Gil Walsh Interiors with an Arts and Crafts green tile, a reproduction of an old fireplace from my reference library.

ABOVE: The spa at Glendorn for massage, manicures, and pedicures, recently added to guest services.

What was originally the living room in the main Lodge at Glendorn has been transformed into the guest dining room using bold colors and patterns. The Lodge was built of redwood, with a cathedral ceiling and a two-story stone fireplace.

A terrace for outdoor dining and relaxing. The design of the Lodge is in keeping with thatched roof houses found in the English countryside. As the Dorn family grew, new cabins and cottages were added to the property, each decorated by a member of the family for their personal use.

FACING: The wine cellar, in the main Lodge, is used for wine tastings and intimate dinners.

ABOVE: The billiards room and bar is done in bold, rich plaids perfect for a country resort. A corner fireplace adds even more warmth to the room.

ABOVE: A small breakfast nook in The Roost, which was the first cabin built on the property by one of the Dorn children for his family.

RIGHT: Partial view of the sitting room leading to the hallway in The Roost. Guests can book individual cabins or the main Lodge. Glendorn serves from 3,500–4,000 guests annually.

A small bedroom in The Roost with a spool bed, oak paneling, and a fireplace with Dutch tiles.

ABOVE: A log structure has been converted into a fish and tackle shop for guests who enjoy fly-fishing in its well-stocked trout streams. Glendorn is an outdoor enthusiast's year-round paradise, with hiking trails, skeet and trap shooting, horseback riding, and cross-country skiing.

OVERLEAF: Porch outside of John's Cabin, with willow furniture and a magnificent view of the lake and the Allegheny National Forest. The property, now a resort, is built on 1,200 acres of wooded land.

Duquesne Club

The Duquesne Club in Pittsburgh is a thirteen-story Romanesque building, the club's home since 1890. The club was originally founded in 1873 in another location by Andrew Carnegie, Henry Clay Frick, Frank B. Laughlin, George Westinghouse Jr. and Henry Phipps, titans of industry and known for their philanthropy—the Carnegie Museum and Library, for example. Originally designed by Longfellow, Alden and Harlow, the club was expanded by Janssen & Cocken in 1931, all noted architects of the time. It has four times been ranked the Number One City Club in the nation and entered the National Register of Historical Places in 1995.

In 1980, women were admitted as members, initially just three, but a beginning. Prior to this, even accompanied by a member, ladies had to use their own entrance, which still exists. I'm glad to say the famous main entrance with its revolving door is used by both sexes today.

In 1984, I was contacted by the club's general manager at the time, Melvin Rex, to begin the redesign of certain areas of the club beginning with the bedrooms, which led to redecorating the public rooms and private suites owned by local corporations. Eventually, the work encompassed all areas of the club, including the addition of a modern spa, gym, and new kitchens. It has the atmosphere of an Edwardian gentlemen's club. The project was enormous in scope. The club has served as a centerpiece for social and business entertaining for decades, but the rules banned the placing of business papers on any table. No doubt scores of deals had been made quietly in private dining room and corporate suites. The entrance and corridors were critical to the design scheme, since they welcomed members and guests for over a century and were important in maintaining this sense of tradition while bringing a

fresh elegance to this Titan's Temple. My work had to speak to a century-old history while inspiring pride in a refreshed classical look.

The logical plan was to begin with the most essential areas, including the entrance and main hallways while I discreetly tackled the guest bedrooms that were not regularly in use and bathrooms desperately in need of updating. The scope of the project could not be done overnight for financial reasons as well as for minimizing interruptions to the flow and use of the club. Melvin Rex and his team, with board approval, devised a plan for which areas we would tackle, resulting in one major project per year over twenty years, concluding in 2005.

Having done the critical public areas of the Main Reading Room and Library Room, I turned my attention to the superbly appointed circa '40s Dining Room, now the Ladies Dining Room. With such a beloved institution, it was essential to maintain the ambience while bringing a modern interpretation to classic design. With high-polished wood columns, we painted the baseboards and wainscoting white to brighten the corridors, giving added life to the burgundy patterned carpet and striped green walls; a mixture of striped silks and tapestry cover the chairs, settees, and benches. The richness of the green and burgundy is relieved with wainscoting and finished with artwork donated over the years by club members.

Times are changing and so is the Duquesne Club. I am now helping to modernize the Reading Room. In today's world, people do business more on electronic devices than the printed page; the club plans to be more member-friendly by relaxing its no-business rule in the Reading Room, an enormous space filled with overstuffed wing-backed chairs and sofas that formerly

Exterior of the thirteen-story Romanesque home of the Duquesne Club since 1890, founded by such titans of industry as Andrew Carnegie, Henry Clay Frick, George Westinghouse, and Henry Phipps, to name a few. It has been a private club since 1873.

permitted only whispered conversations. Since information and news is gathered from iPads, and newspapers are read electronically, the modernization of the Reading Room will allow this underused space to become the hub for computer-savvy executives. A small six-stool bar for coffee, snacks, and drinks will be added to one end of this elegant English drawing room, to be serviced by a newly installed kitchen.

As an interior designer in Pittsburgh for over twenty years, I had the pleasure of working on a number of exquisite properties, including residential mansions and estates, world-famous golf clubs such as Laurel Valley, and the Hunt Stables at Rolling Rock.

Working on the Duquesne Club, which has played host to presidents, including Ulysses S. Grant, and European royalty, appeased my desire to use my classical design background in the English, French, and Italian styles. There is nothing more gratifying than having a client return to me to update a project or begin the interior design of a new home or weekend retreat. When a project represents respecting a historic property, I am even more honored by the confidence placed in me and my team.

TOP LEFT: The Duquesne Club has the atmosphere of an Edwardian gentlemen's club. To brighten the corridor, we painted the baseboard and wainscoting white to offset the rich burgundy patterned carpet and green striped green walls. The chairs, settees, and benches were done in striped silks and tapestry fabrics.

TOP RIGHT: One of the private dining rooms at the club, used for business meetings or intimate dinners, with spectacular views of the city of Pittsburgh.

BOTTOM LEFT: The David M. Roderick Conference Center, which opened in 1988 and is located on the third floor of the club, is set up with the latest in modern technology for presentations.

BOTTOM RIGHT: The Reading Room, which once only permitted whispered conversations and no business papers on the tables, is being updated with a bar for coffee and drinks. It is sure to become the hub for savvy executives using iPads and PDAs to get their news.

LEFT: Patterned Axminster carpets, rich green upholstery, and burgundy walls speak to the English gentlemen's club atmosphere. A view into the Duquesne Room, formerly the Ladies Dining Room, has retained its magnificent crystal chandelier. All the artwork has been donated by members over the years.

ABOVE: The covered-roof garden patio is two stories high and perfect for lunches and cocktail receptions. The French doors lead back into the club. You feel transported to Europe in this superb garden looking up to the second-floor balconies; a hidden treasure you might find in Paris or Rome where great food and wine are served.

Blue on Blue

Modern painter John Ruskin said, *"Blue* color is everlastingly appointed by the deity to be a source of *delight."*

Blue is a magical color that calms my spirit. Both men and women are attracted to this color, which is important in interior design. Blue dates back to the earliest of times in religious imagery and buildings such as the blue mosques of Iran, Egypt, and Turkey. In India, the god Krishna is often depicted with blue skin.

I love visiting museums both here and abroad. The works of art I love reinforce my passion for blue. While attending Chatham College in Pittsburgh, the drama department wanted to do something experimental and selected the play *Desire Caught by the Tail,* written by Pablo Picasso. This unique production had characters without names or costumes. I built and painted the sets and also designed and constructed all the costumes, referencing various periods of Picasso's art for inspiration. The show received rave reviews, but I wound up with a bleeding ulcer on opening night and had to go to hospital. That was a blue period for me! I scored an A+ on my thesis and after graduation realized that I so loved set design that the experience started me on the road to interior design.

Blue stimulates personal thought and insights. Looking up at the sky can bring you peace. Just as nature is an inspiration, so does art—such as works from Picasso's Blue period—play an important role in the way I see color.

Art can often determine a room's color scheme. The blue painting on the wall set the tone for this living room, with its white linen sofa, blue patterned side chairs, and a mix of colorful blue and yellow throw pillows.

Vincent Van Gogh said, "There is no blue without *yellow* and without orange." Renowned painters have inspired how I approach interior design. I see color as they did, but I express it in a three-dimensional way, bringing the color of their paintings into a *living environment* that can be touched and experienced every day.

FACING: Black-and-white photographs of cast from the Picasso play *Desire Caught by the Tail*, where I designed and built all the sets and costumes as my senior thesis from Chatham College in Pittsburgh.

ABOVE: A white linen sofa and marble console face three colorful abstract paintings by the fireplace. The colors of the paintings were picked up in the throw pillows and on the blue-and-white settee to the left.

ABOVE: The reception room at Lost Tree in North Palm Beach.

RIGHT: The colorful living room at a Palm Beach cottage filled with the owner's treasures. The turquoise vintage fabric used on the wicker sofa and chairs picks up the colors of the Hunt Slonem painting over the fireplace.

An elegant sunroom on Martha's Vineyard uses various shades of blue in a floral print and a striped area rug. The fabrics play nicely on white wicker furniture. It's an ideal room for reading or lounging.

A view of my living room on Martha's Vineyard. I took my inspiration from the blue of the sea and sky and the white sandy beach for the color scheme. The blue-and-white abstract carpet is the perfect platform on which to build.

This seaside cottage is an ideal retreat for its owner, a potter whose work can be seen in the painted breakfront. The pale blue sofa matches handsomely with plaid and floral patterns on the chairs, making this a cozy living room for weekend getaways.

A blue lattice rug is a wonderful beginning for this blue-on-blue room. An abstract diamond-patterned fabric is used for the upholstered chairs, with a solid white linen for the sofa. The splash of bright primaries in the painting brings the room together.

Blue generates an emotional response. Think of the anticipation of receiving a Tiffany blue box. It is reported that scientists have successfully used blue light to treat psychological problems. Blue is also the color of verbal communication. The use of various shades of blue in your home communicates the message you want to impart.

I believe every house I design must have blue incorporated in the overall scheme, whether an entire theme for a room or in the use of rugs, window treatments, accent cushions, or upholstery fabrics.

Blue is universal, and these different styles of rooms demonstrate how varied shades of blue can be used in a myriad of ways, from accents to bold backdrops.

One of my favorite French painters, Raoul Dufy, said, "Blue is the only color which maintains its own *character* in all its tones …"

FACING: What an elegant way to enter a mansion in the estate section of Palm Beach. This formal reception hall with its hand-painted old English maritime scene is sure to dazzle. The subtle blue shades of the skirted table and valance are perfect for this neoclassic three-story Regency mansion brought back to life for its new owner.

ABOVE: A more traditional take on an elegant room is this lush dining room in the town of Sewickley, Pennsylvania, with its arresting wallpaper and blue-and-white vases taking center stage. I believe any house I design should incorporate blue in at least one room.

TOP: A subtle blue-and-white duvet and matching headboard on this metal four-poster bed is the perfect way to relax in an environment conducive to a wonderful night's sleep. Blue is a magical color that calms the spirit.

ABOVE: Blue is a color that is liked by both men and women, so it can be ideal for a master bedroom, with blue and white used throughout and contrasted with celadon green walls.

RIGHT: Even a hint of blue can add to the overview of a room. This sweet country bedroom with its walnut four-poster bed is the perfect place to curl up for an afternoon nap.

PREVIOUS OVERLEAF: With Mediterranean blue walls, this master bedroom in south Florida is light and airy, with touches of blue on crisp white linens, duvet, and pillow shams. The four-poster bed introduces a soft cocoa to the room, which carries through to the window treatments.

LEFT: This charming blue room with white twin wicker beds is made even brighter with fun accents of antique blue-and-white quilts and print pillow shams.

ABOVE: As Van Gogh said, "There is no blue without yellow and without orange." This elegant master bedroom illustrates that perfectly.

ABOVE, LEFT: Blue-and-white wallpaper transforms this master bath into a work of art.

ABOVE, RIGHT: The trompe l'oeil creates the illusion of wainscoting in this Palm Beach powder room. A delicate bowl serves as the basin.

FACING: Blue-and-white wallpaper transforms a master bath that is finished with a marble counter and back splash.

Riot of Color

Everything that excites my *imagination* and puts
a *smile* on my face is connected to color.

I adore color. I can't imagine life without it. Color informs everything I do in my personal life and in my interior design work. My fashion background first triggered my love for color—bright, vivid, explosive, refined, subtle or subdued.

The two years I studied fashion design at Bennett College—sketching, draping, and selecting fabrics—was a great foundation for when I turned my attention to interior design. I learned to love fabrics and the myriad of color combinations that can be used in a dress or ensemble. There are solids or blocks of different colors that work so well in combination. A paisley print can bring subtle hues of gray, purple, and green together for just the right way of dressing. The sophisticated look of camel and gray; the mix of blue and brown—all of these combinations work in fashion and also translate beautifully to interior design for homes.

This house in Vero Beach, Florida, is owned by a well-respected artist whose work is colorful and bold. She wanted that same boldness in the interiors of her home, and turquoise walls are the perfect backdrop.

I had the good fortune of designing four homes for an artist whose paintings are filled with color. As opposed to creating a blank canvas that would serve as a backdrop for her art, we used bold colors, such as turquoise on her dining room walls, to complement the art. Some might hesitate to add so much color to a room. As I see it, your home should be a living, breathing space that reflects your bright and lively personality. I say, create a space that embraces you in pleasing colors. While your guests and friends may not remark on your beige or white walls, when you use the right color, they will walk away saying, "Why didn't I think of that?"

When you embrace color, you are harnessing an energy that reflects in your home. Each color tells its own story. Everything starts with nature. I love the extraordinary bounty of colors as spring comes to life, seeing the purple and yellow crocuses popping up and fields of daffodils returning each year around Easter.

FACING: There is a sense of excitement as you enter the living room of this Vero Beach house. We decided on red walls to showcase her art. The mix of reds, yellows, and purples creates an awe-inspiring result. The canvases could have been shown on white or beige walls, but the results would not have been as interesting.

ABOVE: Don't be afraid of color. Bold colors demand bold patterns, as in the black-and-white vertically striped armchairs. Red is one of my favorite colors. The mixture of red, green, and purple creates a strong palette and dramatic effect.

My favorite color is red—a certain shade I like to refer to as Gil Walsh Red. I have a favorite red jacket in my closet that makes me feel great as I walk out the door. Red is said to stimulate and create passion. In the Eastern cultures of India and China, the color is used in marriages. How happy does China red make you feel? It always makes me feel energized.

LEFT: The black-and-white accents, as in the checkerboard floor and backsplash, continue the color scheme of the house. China red cabinets, black marble countertops, and green cushions for the kitchen chairs give a playful touch to this artist's kitchen.

ABOVE: When you sit down to eat, the ambiance starts with the setting of the table. The use of color adds excitement to the anticipation of the meal in the pool area of this Palm Beach mansion.

ABOVE: The formal dining room in this Palm Beach mansion is a bold statement with its coral walls; yet the color brings out the brilliance of handsome furnishings. Coral-and-white drapes complete the room, picking up the colors of the area rug.

FACING: What a nice surprise for guests: the powder room becomes more interesting using the iconic Scalamandré zebra wallpaper for color and whimsy.

On the palest spectrum, yellow can be uplifting. There is a cheerfulness to the color, and in a bedroom it can bring about an atmosphere conducive to a great night's sleep. Yellow—from the palest buttercup to the patina of a Tuscan villa—also contrasts beautifully in a room with blue, orange, green, and red. There are no limits to the shades of yellow, from dusty to brilliant.

FACING: The dining area takes on a whimsical charm as Tuscan yellow walls are paired with blue-and-white-checked chairs. The blue painted breakfront showcases plates and glasses that match the scheme of the room.

ABOVE: Yellow is a cheerful color that is always uplifting. It also contrasts beautifully with a wide range of colors. The yellow walls set the style for other colors and patterns to be combined, like the yellow/green/red plaid sofa, solid coral chairs, and the blue ottoman that doubles as a coffee table.

LEFT: Strong colors are perfect for sunrooms and loggias. Even at night, the room is bright and cheerful. The combination of colors used here is taken from the area rug, which is made of recycled plastic and woven into carpeting that is both great looking and eco friendly.

Green can never be overlooked. Just gaze out your window and see the wide variety of shades of green, from the trees to the grass to the stems of flowers. Green is stable and balanced. In Georgia, they say that it is impossible to number the shades of green that landscape the state. There is a graciousness to green.

ABOVE: A charming guest bedroom has nailhead headboards and crisp white linens bordered in burgundy. The sea creatures add a splash of color.

FACING: Green should never be overlooked. It is a wonderful color in all its various shades. A wrought iron gate ensures a dramatic entrance in this Vero Beach home.

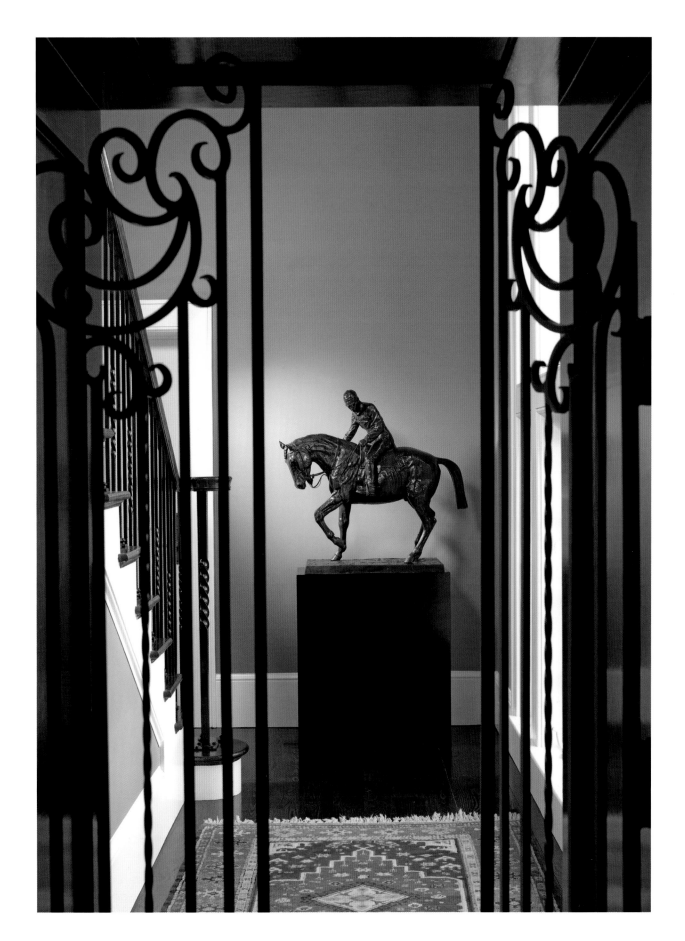

This is a corporate suite for PPG
Paints at the Duquesne Club in
Pittsburgh. The checkerboard wall
is painted with different colors and
used to showcase PPG's consumer
print advertising.

And who could live without blue? I can't downplay the effect that blue can have on life and home, whether it's in a replica of a Ming vase, in an accent pillow for a yellow striped sofa, or a backdrop for a wall in a den or guest cottage. Blue comes from the sky and the sea. It creates the perfect picture of what life can hold: a sunny day, a renewal, or memories of a holiday where the water goes from turquoise to Mediterranean blue to blue-black. Nature made blue the perfect color for our lives.

A combination of colors makes this den an enticing place to be. Starting with royal blue walls, the addition of royal blue, golden yellow, and red in solid and checked upholstered furniture takes its cue from the colors of the rug—a warm and welcoming room to just sit back and relax.

Show Houses

The great compliment to an interior designer is an *invitation* to do a room in a prestigious show house that benefits a *wonderful* charitable organization.

I have been privileged to participate in a number of show houses within the past few years. I was honored to design the living room at the Red Cross Show House in Palm Beach; the 2014 Hampton Designer Show House in Bridgehampton, NY benefiting Southampton Hospital, where I did a tribute to the iconic interior designer, Betty Sherrill. I was among six designers invited to take part in the 2015 Palm Beach Jewelry, Art and Antique Show Designer Showcase.

The dream of every interior designer is an invitation to take part in the Kips Bay Decorator Show House in New York City, in support of the Kips Bay Boys & Girls Club. The room I designed was in the 2016 show house. The centerpiece for my design of the powder room and hallway was a stunning portrait of Jennifer Lopez by celebrity photographer Tony Duran. J. Lo is an alumna of the Boys & Girls Club of New York City. It seemed a most fitting salute to both Kips Bay and Ms. Lopez.

The 2016 Kips Bay Decorator Show House in New York City. Pictured here is the Christopher Leidy photograph entitled *Night Whips.* The ethereal Dandelion chandelier was designed by Tony Duquette, and the artistic wall elements are by Global Views.

FACING: The guest powder room at the 2016 Kips Bay Decorator Show House with celebrity photographer Tony Duran's portrait of Jennifer Lopez reflected in the Baker Folie mirror. J. Lo was one of the many youths who benefited from Kips Bay Boys & Girls Club.

ABOVE: The cabinet is topped with a bronze mirrored crackle glass countertop by Andrew Pearson. Kohler Briolette vessel sink in translucent Doe glass; a Kohler Margaux sink faucet in brushed bronze completes the room.

ABOVE, LEFT: Baker Petalo mirror and Arnault hand-carved console with veneer top by Christopher Guy.

ABOVE, RIGHT: Another view of the Dandelion chandelier designed by Tony Duquette.

FACING: Metal star light fixture designed by Tony Duquette.

ABOVE: For the 2014 Hampton Show House benefiting Southampton Hospital, I chose to do a colorful tribute to the iconic interior designer Betty Sherrill. The room is a mix of bright colors and patterns in reds, lavenders, yellows, and greens. A bold patterned rug adds another design element to the room.

FACING: In a corner of the 2014 Hampton Show House, yellow linen-covered chairs with flounced skirts are accented with needlepoint pillows and a cashmere throw.

OVERLEAF: The Palm Beach Jewelry, Art & Antique Show is one of the most anticipated events of the year; 170 international dealers in art, furniture, and jewelry come to Palm Beach to showcase their merchandise. In the 2015 Designer Showcase, I illustrated lush layering and the bold use of color. The room setting began with a patterned area rug. A fringed sofa lusciously layered in throw pillows, matching brass mirrors, and a striking mix of fabrics, patterns, and art made a strong statement.

Above: The living room of the 2005 Red Cross Show House in Palm Beach.

Facing: Dining area in the 2005 Red Cross Show House.

Acknowledgments

Thanks first to my amazing design team for their talent and limitless enthusiasm; librarian, administration staff, and consultants; they support me every day, in every way, with unconditional love and encouragement that I could not live without.

A special thank-you to all my clients over the years, who trusted me with their most treasured possessions—their homes—and without whom this beautiful book would not be a reality.

Thanks to Andrea Halley-Wright, who handles my social media; to my thousands of followers, who continually respond with their approval and likes; and to the publications that have shown their support by publishing my work.

To everyone who had a hand in the creation and design of this book: all the photographers who captured the spirit and substance of my design in such poignant ways; Steven Stolman, who introduced me to Madge Baird; and everyone at Gibbs Smith who helped to publish *A Case For Color;* and especially Margaret Reilly Muldoon, who has promoted my work for years and whose amazing memory and talent captured my voice.

To my family and everyone at the firm, you inspire and encourage me every day. I am eternally grateful.

Gil Walsh

Photo Credits

Benson, Robert: 22, 23

Brantley, Carmel: 190, 191

Engelbrecht, Roy: 177

Ennis, Phillip: 180, 182, 183, 184, 185

Fisher, Scott: 31, 35, 37, 161

Groover, Joy Lynne: 24, 25

Hamilton, Lori: 114

Hare, Clyde: 138

Little, Christopher: 116, 118, 119, 120, 123

Massery, Ed: 32, 60, 61, 140, 141, 142, 143, 155

Partenio, Michael: 5, 58, 62, 76, 78, 79, 150, 151, 152, 157

Rabinowtiz, Jerry: 81, 82, 83, 100, 101, 102

Sargent, Kim: 2, 4, 5, 6, 8, 10, 18, 20, 21, 26, 27, 28, 29, 30, 32, 33, 34, 36, 38, 40, 41, 42, 43, 44, 45, 46, 47, 48, 49, 50, 51, 52, 53, 54, 55, 56, 57, 63, 64, 65, 66, 67, 68, 70, 71, 72, 73, 74, 75, 80, 85, 86, 88, 89, 90, 91, 92, 93, 94, 95, 96, 97, 98, 104, 106, 107, 108, 109, 110, 111, 112, 113, 124, 126, 127, 128, 129, 130, 131, 132, 133, 134, 135, 136, 144, 147, 148, 149, 153, 154, 156, 158, 160, 162, 163, 164, 166, 167, 169, 170, 171, 172, 173, 174, 175, 178, 186, 187, 188